Fit in the digits

Copy the puzzles on to squared paper.
the numbers so that they fit together
Two numbers have been filled in for you ...

CW00422295

						3
			4	1	6	
						8
						1
						4

5-digit numbers	3-digit numbers	2-digit numbers
36814	416	98
	249	81
4-digit numbers	735	84
	120	74
6438	542	93
8195	251	50
8456	867	96
7860	464	14
6183		23

			2			
5	1	4	6			
			3			
			8			
			9			

5-digit numbers	4-digit numbers	3-digit numbers
96241	8607	306
26389	5038	747
73981	7417	
65922	6872	2-digit numbers
18621	3680	
20392	5146	99
		25
		37
		64
		81
		30

Addition puzzles

5 + 1 + 9
+   +
8   (15)   2
+   +
2 + 9 + 4

The number in the middle is 15 so the rows must have a total of 15.

$$5+1+9=15 \qquad 2+9+4=15$$

The columns must also have a total of 15.

5   9
+   +
8   2
+   +
2   4

Both columns have totals of 15.

Copy and complete.

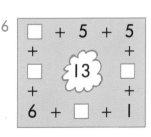

1

7 + □ + 3
+   +
□   (16)   9
+   +
□ + 5 + □

2

□ + 8 + 9
+   +
10   (18)   5
+   +
□ + □ + □

3

□ + □ + □
+   +
6   (20)   8
+   +
9 + □ + 2

4

□ + 7 + 7
+   +
6   (19)   □
+   +
□ + □ + 2

5

4 + 7 + □
+   +
□   (17)   □
+   +
5 + □ + 10

6

□ + 5 + 5
+   +
□   (13)   □
+   +
6 + □ + 1

Investigations

The digits 3, 8 and 2 can be arranged in different ways and added to give these additions:

$3+8+2$ $3+2+8$ $8+2+3$ $8+3+2$ $2+8+3$ $2+3+8$

Each of them can be arranged in two more ways by putting brackets in different places like this:
$3+8+2$ also gives
$(3+8)+2$ and $3+(8+2)$.

$(3+8)+2=11+2=13$ $3+(8+2)=3+10=13$

The two answers are the same.

1　3, 8 and 2 give eighteen different additions.
　　Do you know what the eighteen answers will be?
　　Work them out and see if you were right.

2　Write down the eighteen additions you can obtain
　　from 4, 9 and 1.
　　Do you know what the eighteen answers will be?
　　Work them out and see if you were right.

3　How many different additions can you make from
　　2, 5 and 5?
　　Do you know what the answers will be?
　　Write them down and see if you were right.

4　Investigate how many additions you can make
　　using 6, 4, 7 and 3.
　　You don't *have* to write them all down.
　　Will they all have the same total? If so, what will it be?

Greatest and smallest

| 7 | 9 | 5 | 1 |

Write the numbers 7, 9, 5 and 1 on separate cards.
Using two of the cards the greatest number you can
make is 97.

1 What is the smallest number you can make with two of the
   cards?

2 What is the greatest number you can make with:
   (a) three of the cards?
   (b) all four cards?

3 What is the smallest number you can make with:
   (a) three of the cards?
   (b) all four cards?

4 Arrange the four cards to make an addition using two
   2-digit numbers.
   For example: 59
                     +71
       The sum is 130

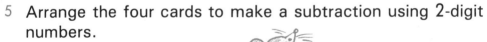

   (a) What is the greatest sum you can make?
   (b) What is the smallest sum you can make?

5 Arrange the four cards to make a subtraction using 2-digit
   numbers.
   For example: 57
                     −19

   The difference is 38

   (a) What is the greatest difference you can make?
   (b) What is the smallest difference you can make?

Investigations

The Greatest Total Game.

You need two players and a referee to play this game.

1 (a) Prepare ten cards, one for each of the digits 0 to 9.

   (b) On a piece of paper, each player needs to draw a table like this:

   (c) The object of the game is to make the largest possible total.

   (d) The referee mixes up the cards and places them face downwards in a pile. He then turns over the first card. Both players write the digit on the card in any place on their tables.

   (e) The referee turns over the next three cards one at a time and the players fill in each digit on their tables.

   (f) Both players now add their 2-digit numbers and the player with the greater total wins and scores 2 points. If the two totals are the same, each player scores I point.

   (g) Take it in turns to be referee and play the game six times, so each person is referee twice. The player with the highest number of points is the winner.

2 Play the game as before, but this time with 3-digit numbers, so the table will be like this: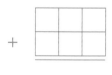

You can use a calculator to help with adding.

Shopping for bargains

1 You only have time to go to one shop. You want to spend
as little money as possible.
Which shop would you go to if you had to buy:
(a) flour, sugar and bread?
(b) bread, margarine, jam and tea?

2 (a) Which is the better bargain, the Star Buy at Star or the
Special Offer at Wavy Stores?
(b) Why do you think shops have Star Buys or Special
Offers?

3 Look at the prices for bread, margarine and jam at Star.
Mike bought 2 of these things.
There are three possible pairs of things he could have
bought.
Use the prices to find their cost.
There are three possible answers. Find them all.

4 (a) What is the total cost if you buy the flour, tea and
sugar at Wavy Stores?
(b) Find the smallest number of coins you could use to pay
for them.

Code making and breaking

1   Make up a code that uses addition and subtraction.
    Make up a message for a friend to decode.
    You decode your friend's message.

2   You are only given the first four letters of these codes.
    Find out what numbers the other letters of the alphabet
    have.
    (a) A 3, B 7, C 11, D 15 ...
    (b) A 140, B 137, C 134, D 131 ...
    (c) A $\frac{1}{2}$, B 1, C 1$\frac{1}{2}$, D 2 ...

3   This one is more difficult so you have been given more
    letters. Can you work out the rest?
    A 1, B 2, C 4, D 7 .... J 46, K 56 .....

4   Find out about codes.
    Why are they needed?
    How do they work?

5   ?sedoc ekil ouy od

More codes to solve

Code	A	B	C	D	E	F	G	H	I	J	K	L	M
	20	16	6	10	18	3	12	8	30	50	4	28	15

N	O	P	Q	R	S	T	U	V	W	X	Y	Z
35	14	40	9	5	24	21	27	1	25	11	7	13

1 What has teeth, but no mouth?

4 × 5		3 × 2	2 × 7	5 × 3	8 × 2

2 What would you do if your baby sister swallowed your ball point pen?

3 × 9	4 × 6	6 × 3		2 × 10

10 × 4	9 × 2	5 × 7	6 × 1	3 × 10	4 × 7

3 How do you start a race for jellies?

4 × 3	3 × 6	3 × 7		8 × 3	2 × 9	7 × 3

4 They have twelve legs, six ears but no eyes. Who are they?

3 × 7	2 × 4	9 × 2		7 × 3	4 × 2	5 × 1	3 × 6	2 × 9

4 × 4	7 × 4	5 × 6	7 × 5	2 × 5		3 × 5	10 × 3	2 × 3	6 × 3

A riddle

When does a river get angry?

Divide, then decode the riddle.
$12 \div 4 = 3$. The letter given in the decoder for 3 is W.

1	$12 \div 4 = \underline{3}\ \vert\ \text{W}$
2	$27 \div 3 = \underline{\quad\vert\quad}$
3	$24 \div 4 = \underline{\quad\vert\quad}$
4	$25 \div 5 = \underline{\quad\vert\quad}$

5	$14 \div 2 = \underline{\quad\vert\quad}$
6	$40 \div 5 = \underline{\quad\vert\quad}$
7	$20 \div 2 = \underline{\quad\vert\quad}$
8	$30 \div 5 = \underline{\quad\vert\quad}$
9	$24 \div 3 = \underline{\quad\vert\quad}$
10	$20 \div 4 = \underline{\quad\vert\quad}$
11	$18 \div 3 = \underline{\quad\vert\quad}$

12	$0 \div 2 = \underline{\quad\vert\quad}$
13	$10 \div 5 = \underline{\quad\vert\quad}$
14	$32 \div 4 = \underline{\quad\vert\quad}$
15	$35 \div 5 = \underline{\quad\vert\quad}$
16	$21 \div 3 = \underline{\quad\vert\quad}$
17	$12 \div 2 = \underline{\quad\vert\quad}$
18	$28 \div 4 = \underline{\quad\vert\quad}$

19	$3 \div 3 = \underline{\quad\vert\quad}$
20	$16 \div 4 = \underline{\quad\vert\quad}$

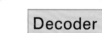

Decoder										
0	1	2	3	4	5	6	7	8	9	10
C	I	R	W	T	N	E	S	O	H	M

Find the sign

When solving problems you need to know whether to add, subtract, multiply or divide. You do not need to know the actual numbers to be able to decide what to do.

For example: there are ■ boys and each has ● comics. How many comics are there?

You need to **multiply** (● × ■).

What would you need to do (add, subtract, multiply or divide) to find the answer to each of these problems?

1 ■ boys and ● girls. How many children?

2 ■ books; ● on each shelf. How many shelves are needed?

3 ■ pigs on a farm; ● in each sty. How many sties?

4 ■ egg boxes; ● eggs in each box. How many eggs?

5 ■ children in a class; ● go out to play. How many are left?

6 ■ words in a line; ● lines on a page. How many words on a page?

7 ■ apples cost ● pence each. What is the total cost?

8 A bag of apples cost ■ pence. There are ● apples in the bag. What is the cost of one apple?

9 Make up some other questions, using ■ and ●, that involve division.

Find the sign

Rewrite the equation using $+$, $-$, $\times$ or $\div$ instead of ● to make the correct answer.

$(9 ● 2) ● 4 = 7$

$(9 + 2) - 4 = 11 - 4 = 7$

Now try these.

1 $(10 ● 3) ● 2 = 32$

2 $7 ● (18 ● 13) = 35$

3 $8 ● (1 ● 4) = 40$

4 $15 ● (9 ● 3) = 42$

5 $(50 ● 5) ● 10 = 0$

6 $7 ● (13 ● 9) = 28$

7 $16 ● (4 ● 4) = 32$

8 $(7 ● 3) ● 60 = 81$

9 $32 ● (6 ● 1) = 38$

10 $70 ● (10 ● 2) = 50$

11 $(25 ● 5) ● 2 = 10$

12 $9 ● (40 ● 5) = 17$

13 $10 ● (10 ● 2) = 30$

14 $(56 ● 4) ● 10 = 50$

Copy these and put in your own brackets and signs to make them correct.

15 $26 ● 4 ● 7 = 29$

16 $● 19 ● 11 ● 5 = 6$

17 $14 ● 32 ● 4 = 22$

18 $16 ● 4 ● 3 = 12$

19 $45 ● 5 ● 3 = 3$

20 $9 ● 4 ● 10 = 26$

Designer sums

Using all three digits 7, 6 and 2 with $+$ and $-$ signs you can make these numbers:

$7+6+2=15$ $7+6-2=11$ $7-6+2=3$

$76-2=74$ $62+7=69$ $72+6=78$

You can use brackets if you want to.

1   Make these numbers with 7, 6, 2 $+$, $-$ and brackets.
    (a) **65**   (b) **33**   (c) **19**   (d) **55**   (e) **1**

2   With the same rules as before make as many numbers as you can using 1, 4, 9, $+$, $-$ and brackets. Remember you must use all three digits.

3   Now change the rules.
    You can use one, two *or* three digits. You can use $+$, $-$ and brackets but you don't have to use all of them.
    Use these rules and the digits 3, 5 and 8 to make as many numbers as you can.

The winning number

Follow the changes to find out the number of the winning raffle ticket.

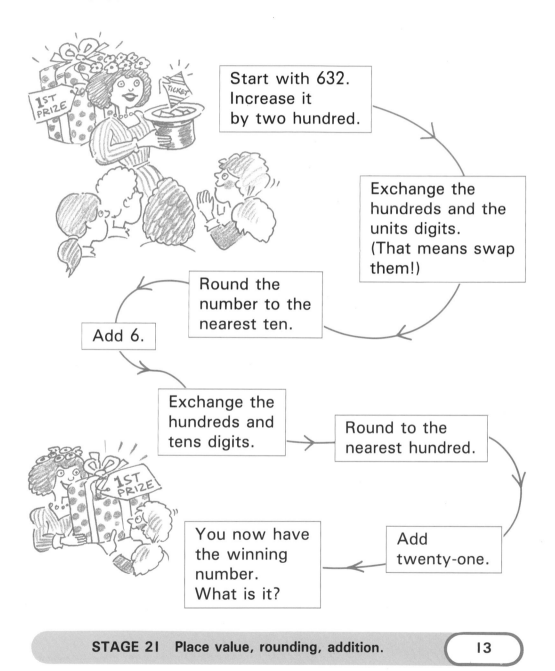

Start with 632.
Increase it
by two hundred.

Exchange the
hundreds and the
units digits.
(That means swap
them!)

Round the
number to the
nearest ten.

Add 6.

Exchange the
hundreds and
tens digits.

Round to the
nearest hundred.

You now have
the winning
number.
What is it?

Add
twenty-one.

Using subtraction

If you like, you may use your calculator to help with these problems.

Subtraction is needed to solve many real-life problems.

Here is one example:
A school was trying to raise £500 for charity. First they had a sponsored walk and raised £134. How much did they still have to raise?

$$
\begin{array}{r}
{}^{4}\cancel{5}{}^{9}\cancel{0}{}^{1}\cancel{0} \\
£500 \\
-£134 \\
\hline
£366 \\
\end{array}
$$

Now try these.

1 How old will you be in the year 2000?

2 How many children are there in your school?
   Find the number of boys. Subtract to find the number of girls.

3 How many pages are there in your maths Textbook?
   How many pages have you completed?
   How many have you still to do?

4 How many days are there until the end of this month? (If today is the last day of the month, how many days are there until the end of next month?)

5 Find some other problems that need to be solved with subtraction.
   Make up some questions and see if your friends can solve them.

Finding shapes

1 Make a list of all the objects in the picture that are close to triangles, squares, circles and rectangles.

2 Look around your classroom. What objects can you see that have triangles, squares, circles or rectangles? List them.

3  These two triangles are the same size and shape. How many **different** triangles can you make?

Investigations into squares

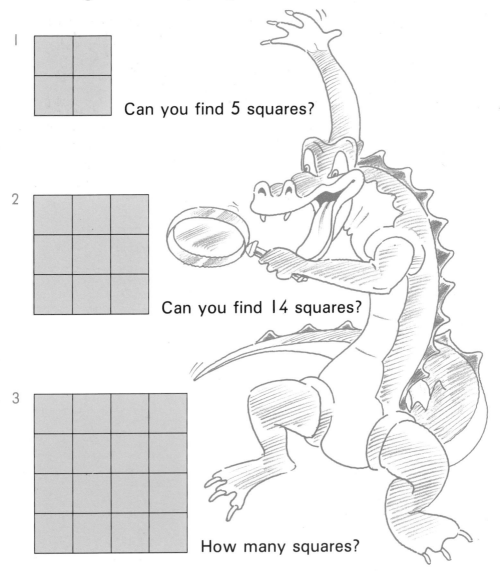

1   Can you find 5 squares?

2   Can you find 14 squares?

3   How many squares?

4   What will the next picture be?
     How many squares will it have?

You're nicked!

The time by my watch was [clock] when I started my patrol. 17 minutes later I saw the accused loitering outside the jewellers. I watched him for 14 minutes and then saw him go inside. 7 minutes later he ran from the shop. I chased him for 25 minutes and caught him hiding behind a very fat lady. I called the Station and a Panda car arrived 9 minutes later. We took the accused to the Station the journey taking 7 minutes. The suspect was cautioned and then interviewed This took 35 minutes. The man was then charged with robbery.

1 What was the time when the accused:
   (a) went into the shop?
   (b) ran from the shop?
   (c) was caught?

2 At what time was the man charged?

3 The clock in the police station was 8 minutes fast. What time did it show:
   (a) when the suspect arrived at the police station?
   (b) when he was charged?

Finding fractions

1   Draw four flowers.
Colour $\frac{1}{2}$ of them red.
Colour $\frac{1}{4}$ of them yellow.
Colour the rest blue.
What fraction is blue?

2   Draw six apples.
Colour $\frac{1}{3}$ of them green.
Colour $\frac{1}{2}$ of them yellow.
Colour the rest red.
What fraction is red?

3   Draw eight leaves.
Colour $\frac{1}{4}$ of them green.
$\frac{1}{4}$ of them brown and
$\frac{1}{4}$ of them yellow.
What fraction is coloured?
What fraction is not coloured?
What fraction is not green?

4   Make up a story with 'a quarter' in it.
Draw a picture about your story.

A fractions game

Draw 16 dots arranged in a square
like this:

Rules   Start at any dot.
You can go through a point more than once.
You can draw lines to join dots upwards or
downwards $|$, and sideways •—•.
You can't draw lines diagonally like this ╱ or ╲.
You mustn't draw over a line that is already drawn.
You mustn't take your pencil off the paper.

Object   To draw as many squares and parts of squares as
possible.

Score   1 point for every complete square.

$\frac{3}{4}$ of a point for three sides of a square.

$\frac{1}{2}$ of a point for two sides of a square.

•—• $\frac{1}{4}$ of a point for one side of a square.

Example   The score is
$\frac{3}{4} + 1 + \frac{1}{2} + \frac{3}{4} + 1 + 1 + \frac{1}{2} + 1 + \frac{1}{2} = 7$

Find your highest score.
Challenge your friends to beat it.

Find a Class Champion.

Now try with 25 dots.

Last one wins

This game is for two players.

One player should draw the grid above on squared paper. The sides of your small squares should be 2 cm. Cut along the thick lines to make 5 black pieces and 5 oranges pieces, one colour for each player.

The other player should draw a similar square with sides of 12 cm and made up of 36 small squares, each with sides of 2 cm. Don't draw the thick lines.

This is the grid.

The players take it in turns to put one of their pieces on to the grid.

Each piece must fit along the lines inside the square and none of the pieces can overlap.

The last player to place a piece wins the game.

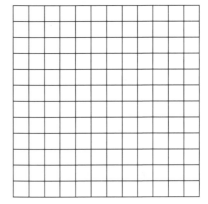

Division using your calculator

You can use your calculator to divide even when there are remainders.

This example will show you how.

Discuss it with your teacher if you are not sure about it.

Example

Divide 28 by 3. What is the remainder?

Enter $\boxed{2}$ $\boxed{8}$ $\boxed{\div}$ $\boxed{3}$ $\boxed{=}$ in your calculator.

The display will show $\boxed{9.3333333}$

This shows $28 \div 3$ is a bit more than 9.

Multiply 9 by 3, $9 \times 3 = 27$, so $27 \div 3 = 9$.

$28 - 27 = 1$ so $28 \div 3 = 9$ R 1. (The remainder is 1).

You can use this method for any numbers, no matter how large they are.

1 Copy and complete this division.

Divide 241 by 9.

Enter $\boxed{2}$ $\boxed{4}$ $\boxed{1}$ $\boxed{\div}$ $\boxed{9}$ $\boxed{=}$ and the display shows

Multiply 26 by 9 and the answer is _____.

$241 -$ _____ $= 7$. So $241 \div 9 =$ _____, R 7.

2 Now do these divisions, giving your answers with a remainder.

(a) $29 \div 4$ (b) $38 \div 5$ (c) $97 \div 10$ (d) $83 \div 3$ (e) $93 \div 6$
(f) $100 \div 7$ (g) $161 \div 8$ (h) $203 \div 9$.

3 Make up some divisions of your own. Find the answers by the method given above. You can divide by larger numbers, for example $311 \div 13$.

Estimating and Measuring

Copy the table. Estimate the lengths of the parts shown in the drawings. Fill in the first column. Now measure the lengths and fill in the second column. How well did you do?

	Estimated length in cm	Measured length in cm
(a)		
(b)		
(c)		
(d)		
(e)		
(f)		
(g)		
(h)		

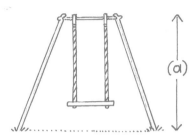

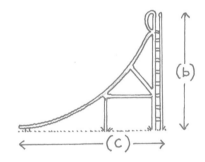

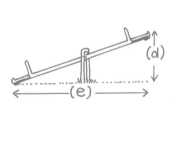

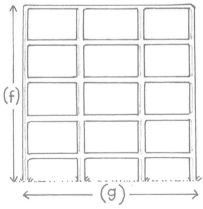

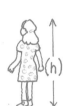

This is a game to test your skill at estimating length.

You need a ruler or a tape measure.

Work with one or more friends.

Write down your estimates for the length of the line AB.
Give your estimates to the nearest half centimetre.

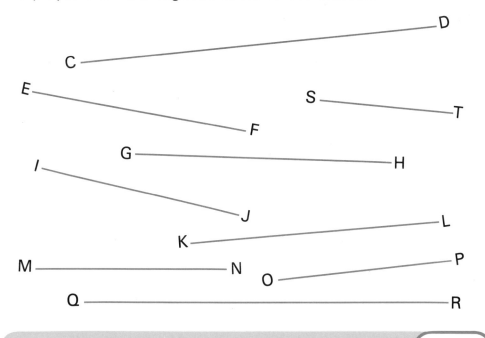

Now measure AB.

Score 5 points for an exact answer, score 4 points for an answer within $\frac{1}{2}$ cm of the correct length, score 3 points within 1 cm, 2 points within $1\frac{1}{2}$ cm, 1 point within 2 cm. Other answers score 0.

Do the same for each of the other lines on this card. The player with the highest score is the winner.

Using a map

Cathy and Steve are travelling from their home to the beach. The map shows the distances in kilometres between their house, the nearby villages (marked ●), and the beach.

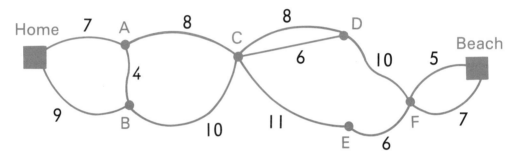

1 (a) How far is it from home to village C if they travel through A?
   (b) How much further would it be if they went through B?

2 (a) What is the shortest distance from home to village D?
   (b) Which villages do they travel through?

3 How far from the beach are they when they are C? Give the shortest distance.

4 What is the shortest distance from home to the beach.?

5 Find the difference between the distances from C to F if one distance is measured through D (by the longest route) and the other through E.

Measuring curves

You can measure the
perimeter of curved
shapes by using
cotton or thin string.

Find the perimeters of these shapes. Give your answers to the
nearest centimetre.

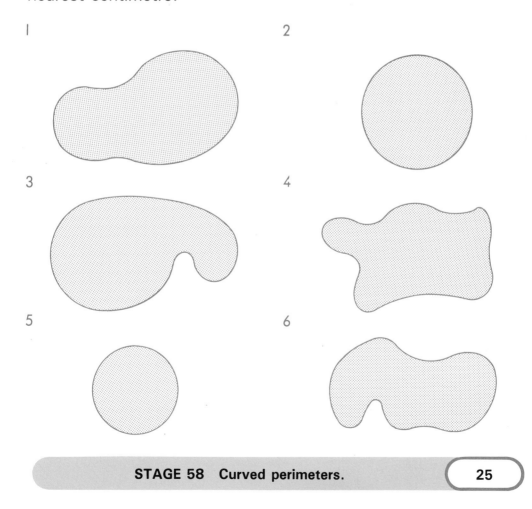

1

2

3

4

5

6

How heavy?

You need a balance and ten 100 gram weights.

1 Hold a book in one hand. With your other hand, pick up 100 gram weights one at a time until you think the weights weigh the same as the book. They may not balance exactly but get as close as you can.
Now use the balance to see if your estimate was right.

2 Work with a friend. Find another book that you estimate weighs, say 300 grams. Ask your friend to estimate the weight. Now weigh the book and see who was nearest.

3 You and your friend each need a large plastic bag and some sand. You should both put sand into your bags until you think the sand and the bag together weigh 400 grams. Use the balance to check your answers.
Who was nearest?

4 Repeat question 3 with other weights.

Investigations

1　You have a container full of water. How can you find the
　weight of the water?
　Weigh the container when it is empty and weigh it when it
　is full of water. Now you can calculate the weight of the
　water.
　How did you do it?
　What was the answer?

2　Fill the container with sand. Use the method in question 1
　to calculate the weight of the sand.

3　Do the same with beads (or buttons, or counters).

4　(a)　If you put the following materials into containers of the
　　　same size, which do you think will be the heaviest:
　　　sand, flour, water, paint, earth or plasticine? Do it!
　(b)　What do you think the order of weight will be starting
　　　with the lightest?
　(c)　Check your answer to (b) by weighing.
　(d)　How would you check it with a balance?

5　Which weighs more: a kilogram of feathers or a kilogram of
　nails?

What day is it?

1 The letters in the days of the week have been mixed up.
Sort them out.

(a) SADYUTE (b) AYRFID (c) DANMOY (d) NUDASY
(e) YATHSURD (f) SEANDDEWY (g) YASTRAUD
(h) Now write them in order, starting with Monday.

2 Sort out the letters to make the months of the year.

(a) YAM   (b) ENJU   (c) CHARM
(d) MEDBREEC   (e) RILPA   (f) NAJYRAU
(g) STUGAU   (h) ROVEBMEN   (i) LYJU
(j) ROTBOCE   (k) BERRYUFA   (l) BERTSPEEM
(m) Now write them in order.

3 What is your favourite day? Why?

4 What is your favourite month? Why?

5 In which month is:
(a) Easter?
(b) Christmas Day?
(c) your school sports day?

6 The earth turns once every
24 hours on its axis.
Find out what this has to do
with **leap years**.

What do I need to know?

There are four problems in column A, but you need to know one more fact to solve each problem.
For each problem find the fact you need from column B then write out the complete problem and solve it.

Column A

Column B

The problems

The missing facts

1 William worked for 4 hours. How much money did he earn?

| William is a teacher. |
| He works 8 hours in 2 days. |
| He is paid £5 an hour. |

2 Julie bought some pencils. She spent 45p. How many pencils did she buy?

| She has less than £1 to spend. |
| Each pencil costs 5p. |
| Pens cost 15p. each. |

3 Clare bought 5 boxes of jam tarts. How many jam tarts did she have?

| The tarts will last for 5 days. |
| 5 people can have 1 tart each. |
| There are 5 tarts in each box. |

4 John earned £6 this week. How much was he paid an hour?

| He normally works 6 hours a week. |
| He worked 3 hours last week. |
| He worked 2 hours this week. |

Investigations into age

Age 35   Age 9

(a) How old will the father be when his son is 16?
(b) How old will the son be when his father is 40?

Age ?   Age 9

(a) The mother is 4 times as old as her daughter. How old is the mother?
(b) How old was the mother when her daughter was born?

Age ?   Age 42

(a) The mother was 28 years old when her son was born. How old is the mother?
(b) What will the difference in their ages be in 5 years time?

Age 55   Age ?

(a) The father was 33 when his daughter was born. How old is the daughter?
(b) What was the difference in their ages 5 years ago?

Think!

Here are some puzzle questions.
Look at them carefully.
You have been warned!

1 Ten posts are to be put up in a straight line with two metres between each post.

What will the distance be between the first and the last post?

2 Katy is 2 years old and her brother, Andy, is 14 years old. How many years will it be before Andy is exactly twice as old as Katy?

3

There was an elephant in front of an elephant, an elephant behind an elephant, and an elephant in the middle.
What is the smallest possible number of elephants?

4 Jenny has twice as many books as Martin. They have 24 books altogether. How many books have they each got?

Think some more!

Here are some more puzzles.

|

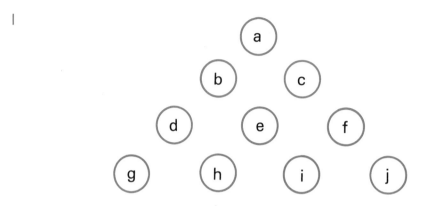

Put ten counters (or coins) on a table to make a triangle.
You have to form a triangle that is the other way up by only
moving three counters. Use the letters to explain how you
did it.

2

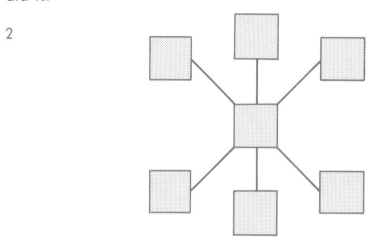

Copy the diagram. You have to put I, 2, 3, 4, 5, 6 and 7 into
the squares so that the total of three squares in a line is the
same for all three lines.